Still Standing
and

Destined for Greatness

From Affirmations to Declarations

ISBN 978-0-578-80664-8

LCCN 2020923042

Dedication

To those who thought their life was over, but

realized it had just begun

Foreword
How Affirmations Changed Me

Affirmations were introduced to me once I separated from my marriage and I am so glad that it was. During this time, I started to read a lot of self-help books and listen to motivation and inspiration to make it through the day. Dealing with the loss of my marriage was a time when I felt extremely small, like I had failed, like I was nothing, I had to rebuild, no, in all honesty create my self-esteem, find my self-worth because for so long I did not have any. I had to move my family and start my life over from scratch, or at least it felt that way. Once I moved into a new space I placed affirmations everywhere I could look, from when I walked into my home, to my bathroom so that I could read something positive every morning before I started my day. Affirmations give you a sense of well-being, it is personal, and it builds your self-esteem if you are actually committed to repeating and believing. Affirmations changed the way I looked at myself, I repeated until I believed it that is why I am so adamant about teaching others to do the same. Repeat it until you believe it, write it down until it is in scripted in your brain.

Andrese

1

Introduction

As I state often, life is a journey that we all must travel, regardless of if we want to or not. Unfortunately, we never know what we are going to go through, what burdens we may have to carry, what loses we will endure and because we are not in control of every aspect of our lives we may become weary and some may lose interest in living the best of their lives because of the concern of the "what if's". What will happen if the wrong decision is made or if there is a complete curve ball in the plans they had for their lives? What happens if you lose someone you love who is never to return or go through a divorce when you thought you had found the person you were destined to spend forever with. How you react to a situation determines the outcome. What if you lose all your material possessions? Do you throw in the towel or continue to persevere? In all honesty what happens, is completely up to you.

A challenge in life should not break you or cause you to give up on yourself. We should not allow a challenge, a hurt, a disappointment or a failure to keep us from seeing the greatness within. Life can get messy and sometimes we cannot see our way through the mess, but if you change your mindset to believe that there is a lesson somewhere in the mess that is going to help me in the long run, you will find it and you will come out stronger. You will find yourself still standing – ready to take full possession of the greatness that was always there.

There is something to learn from everything, and I mean everything - the good, the bad and the ugly. Sometimes we may have to look within ourselves to determine if we ourselves may be the problem causing the mess, the unnecessary challenge, holding onto the disappointment or unhealed from the hurt. Maybe there is something that must be changed within ourselves to reach our life goals and to ultimately find peace and happiness.

Have you ever heard the word "Broken" being used to describe a person who has lost themselves because of some tragic event or hurt that has happened in their life? Well, to be broken does not mean that you cannot fix your life so that you can feel complete again, it just means first wanting it and second putting in the work. There is nothing that comes to you without you doing some work to achieve it and that includes your healing.

We are all ***Destined for Greatness***, no matter our challenges, our hurts, our failures, or our life disappointments. God gave us all the tools we need to live a successful life; it is all up to us what we do with those tools. Learning to use affirmations, ways to remind ourselves that we have value even when we have been broken by life, is a sure way to living victoriously and walking in the greatness God designed as our destined place. Are you ready to take this journey? Do you want to know what it takes? Take this next level journey with me as we declare that we are destined for greatness.

When being destined is not enough to stand

Destined means "certain to meet or intended for". If you are destined that means that something is meant just for you and you shall conquer anything that tries to keep you from what is intended for you. But being destined is not enough, you need a destination. You need to know where you are going so you can determine a path, a plan, and get direction on how to arrive at that destination.

No journey is easy. You must pack, prepare, get ready and then, most importantly, you got to make a move to go. That requires that you unpack one very important thing from your mind: *fear of failure*. Whoever went on a trip that required an airplane ride when they had a fear of flying? Whoever got in a boat to go sailing when they were afraid of water? Fear will hold you hostage to your right now, right here. Fear must be unpacked and traded in for faith in yourself.

It has not been easy at all to stand and walk into greatness, let me share with you once again my journey. I lost my Mom to cancer at 12, the first hurt I ever encountered, to lose my Mom, who was my everything, was and still is the hardest thing I have ever lived through, not even the abuse adds up to losing someone that not only you loved but loved you unconditionally. There is no love like a mother's love. I thought I had found love as a junior in high school, but that turned out to be toxic, I experienced abuse by someone who I thought cared about me and at that time I did not really understand what I had gotten myself into or knew how to love myself enough to seek the help I needed to walk away until I had a reason to. I was pregnant by the age of 17, a senior in high school. Once I had my daughter and the abuse continued, I had to find a way out for the sake of my child, I loved someone more than I loved myself and she was depending on me to keep her safe, so being a Mom gave me strength.

Every journey or every road we take in life will not be fun but I would rather take the trip, go through every obstacle than to sit dormant because you never know what is out there that can impact and change your life for the good wither it is temporary enjoyment or permanent. I want to learn from every experience even the ones that try to break my spirit. I believe that there is a lesson in everything; and taking even an inch of positive can overpower any negative. With all that being said, I have been hit hard in life, from the loss of a parent, to abuse, teen motherhood, single motherhood, divorce, low self-esteem, depression, anxiety, my list can go on and on but one thing that I know for certain is that I never had the desire to give up, yes I may lay low for a minute but giving up has never been an option. I understand that life is not perfect, I still fight battles every day, but I know that my life has purpose and I have places to go and so do you.

2
Destined to Overcome Fear and Failure

A person can quit on themselves and give up on pursuing their dreams because of the fear of failure. Let's talk about that word "FEAR". Everyone has a fear, whether they admit it or not, everyone is scared of something. And if we tell the truth, some fear is healthy and prevents reckless harm to us mentally, physically, and spiritually. But there is an unhealthy fear can steal your joy and ambition, it can cause you to feel that nothing will work out in your favor so why try. It is something that we have made up to be real in or minds and requires a mindset adjustment. Now, some of us may have some valid fears or at least to us they are. Yet, if we do the work and soul search, we can determine when that fear becomes unhealthy and is getting in the way of our greatness.

If I may be transparent, I FEAR dogs. I have no idea why but that has not stopped me from allowing my children to have a dog and I have done it twice. I didn't allow the fear to have complete control of my life, nor did I impose my fears on others. I could have allowed my personal fear to affect my children, but I chose to face and overcome my fear. If I allowed my fear to overcome me, I would have instilled in my children's' minds that dogs were vicious, mean, and scary because of my PERSONAL fear. I could have allowed something that was very real to me impact those closest to me. We were not given the spirit of fear, think on that every time fear stops you from moving forward in life.

Do it scared!

That one thing that you are afraid to try, pursue, or jump into is possibly the one move that will change your life for the better. It is good to take risk and challenge yourself to live beyond your fear. You should jump out there and do whatever it is that you have a desire to do that but causes you to be afraid, no matter what that fear may be, fear of failure or the fear of what others may think, you never know if that one thing that scares you to death may be the one thing that will take you to a whole new level unless you get out there and try it. It is a fact that anything new can cause fear and can be extremely terrifying. We become so comfortable in our daily routines that the thought of trying something new gives palpitations, stress, and anxiety. To move forward you have to combat whatever is causing the fear and the negative energy because nothing comes from your comfort zones.

Think on this, those things that you are now comfortable with were at one point in your life something new. You want to live a life of adventure, purpose, and prosperity and how do you do that, by doing it scared. Whatever scares you the most give it a try, if it doesn't work out at least you tried, as I often say "I would rather have an OOPS than a What If" I can name so many things that I was afraid to do from starting a new job to speaking in public, I promise you that speaking in public or even in small groups still gives me anxiety and makes my heart feel like it is jumping out of my chest but I know that once I start that anxiety will ease up and I know where I want to go in life and what I want to do and that is to share my story of victory and being an overcomer with others who feel lost in hopes that it will change their lives and give them hope and belief in themselves. Every time I get up to speak it does become easier, this is coming from someone who prefers to hid in the background and be invisible, God says not so, I have work for you to do and I want to follow my calling.

I believe that God was preparing me for something greater, he was preparing me to come out of my shell and share with others my testimony. Sometimes He uses others to push you to grow and step out of our comfort zones and place you where you are supposed to be. God places people in our lives who believes in us when we do not believe in ourselves or our own abilities, He puts us in a place where we can grow and be supported without us even knowing the purpose of why am I here. I can remember joining a church some years ago and the Pastor asked me to read the announcements each Sunday morning during service in front of the whole congregation, just talking about it gave me anxiety because remember I said I do not like speaking in public, I do not even like being seen and to stand alone in front of a group of people was terrifying for me and my Pastor knew this so why would he task me with something that would cause me such anguish especially knowing that I am the quietist one in the church. I believe now that this all was preparing me for what I am doing today and helping me in finding my voice to share myself with others with no fear. Every Sunday for years I did it scared, I got up in front of people and gave those announcements until it became natural to me, so natural that I started adding my own twist to it such as giving a word of the week to motivate and inspire others. Your fear may not be talking in public, it could be something totally different like starting a new business, the fear that no one will support you or the fear of starting a new relationship after a divorce or breakup, I can surely relate to that, but you have to move on.

I will remove any fear that is trying to stop me from growing and reaching my full potential or from loving and being loved in return. Never think that because one relationship is over that you cannot move on and find another, I do not believe for a minute that we are meant to be alone and if one relationship fails they are all doomed to fail. One thing I do believe is that we grow through every relationship we have, either we grow together, or we grow apart due to growing. I also believe that we get something out of even the relationships that failed, I was in one relationship where I learned how to love and appreciate myself more, and I learned how to enjoy the finer things, and had some new experiences that I had never encountered in my past relationships like eating fine dining, taking trips to new places, it opened up a whole new world for me.

Although that relationship ended, I am grateful for it because of the new things that I learned about myself and I am very opened to learning more by experiencing time with someone else who may have a whole different lifestyle and learn more about myself, you never know what you will enjoy until you're introduced to it, I had no idea I would like sushi or Thai food until it was introduced to me. Do not allow your fears to keep you from learning more about yourself. Be open to new possibilities you never know where they will take you.

Failure is another misconception that is related to fear. We think if we fail at something our whole life is over when it is not. Can you imagine if we stopped trying to walk after the first fall? It's not even in our minds to stop – no matter how many times we fall, the desire to walk upright overrides any fear or failure that would try to stop us and that's before we turn 2 years old! I understand that no one wants to fail including me, but once again we must change our minds and realize that failure is sometimes what is needed in order to reach success. Failing is not falling over and over again, it's when you won't get back up. It is the getting back up after failed attempts that makes you a winner. Failure is something that one may have to endure on their road trip to reaching their goals, to being successful. Do not stop at the fear and failure destination, keep moving to greatness.

I am destined to overcome fear and failure.

3
Destined to Exist on Purpose

Purpose is the reason something exists. Your existence
has a purpose, we are all here on this earth for a reason.
Although you may not immediately know what your
purpose in life is or the reason why you were created,
if you keep living as well as growing, you will
eventually run into it. Your purpose is what brings you
joy and happiness. If it is a skill of some sort, it will
not be complicated for you and you can get through it
with ease. Your purpose creates meaning, it is your
determination to do or achieve something that is
meaningful. It will be the reason you get up every
morning, it shapes your goals, offers you direction, and
uplifts your mood. Your purpose will be unique to you
and not everyone will understand your dreams and that
will be okay. Your purpose will become your
motivation, it will help you to focus on what is
important to you and your life. When you are able to
answer the questions - why am I here, what do I have

to offer, who am I? - you have found your purpose. Purpose is about finding your gift and using it to help someone else and impact the world in a positive way.

It is important to find your purpose in order to find meaning in life, FOR YOU, FIRST. You must be able to live your life in a way that satisfies you, that's how you find your true happiness. It seems that I spent so many years worrying about what others thought of me, what they would say and how they would view me and how I could make others happy and satisfied with decisions about my life. So much so that I lost focus on my purpose in life and that should have never been the case. I would always advise you to make your own decisions in life in hopes that you would make the best choices. When you find your purpose, you find who you are and you will become so focused on fulfilling your dreams and accomplishing your goals that the opinions of others will not phase you. You become more confident in yourself because you know that you are here for a reason and your influence on others matter. You will be able to affirm yourself, and your greatness, even if and when no one else can see it.

Not everyone has the same purpose, and not everyone has the same gift. There are some people that can do incredible things that no one else on the planet can do but that is their gift, it's important that you find your gift that will fulfill your purpose and be fulfilled with doing everything with that gift that you can.

Unfortunately, sometimes it takes tragedy to find your purpose. A struggle or a hurt happens in your life and pushes you to find who you are and what you have to give. Our purpose at times comes from our pain. When I think of my purpose, I realize that it came from painful experiences in my life. These experiences produced my purpose which is to share my story with others in an effort to help them to deal with the same situations I had to endure and come out on the other side empowered to stand.

My purpose is my truth and the ability to be transparent in that truth. These painful experiences push me deeper into my purpose, but my ability to freely share those experiences with others in hope that they will see a way out of what is damaging them, is the impact of that purpose. For some, purpose may sneak up out of nowhere, you will one day just realize that this is what I am meant to do. For some, purpose will be pushed on them by someone else who can see their potential and what they hold inside that can give hope to their lives and in return someone else's. You may not realize that what you have, the talent that you possess, can be a blessing to someone else.

For example, a singer may not know that their voice brings a sense of calmness, can relieve stress, or even lift another's spirit. Music is therapy. That can be your purpose, to bring life to someone else through song. To find your purpose you must try new things and get out of your own way. It is a fact that we can often miss our purpose by being afraid to try new things, to step out of our comfort zones, to stand out. To step out of your comfort zone does take a level of courage but you must stop thinking and start doing to move forward and progress. Start taking steps to what you want to do in life, if you want to be a singer take lessons. If you want to be a writer, write more. Working towards your purpose should bring you happiness because it is something that you enjoy. Your passion will turn into your purpose in life and you will enjoy every moment of fulfilling it every day.

And do not let your age get in the way. Remember, you were born with a purpose and until it is used up, it is never too late. It does not matter your age at all when you are destined to find your purpose, your reason for existing.

A lot of people have discovered their talent, their motivation, what they are extremely good at, when they were very young, and they just continued to grow in that gift. It is no secret that your gift will make room for you, and it does not matter how many people have the same skill, talent, or ability each one of us operate differently. No singer has the exact same voice, yet each voice is absolutely incredible in its own way. Your gift can be the same as the next person, but it is all in how you operate yours.

Giving up on finding what drives you should never be an option but be sure that once you find that one thing you continue to elevate.

I am destined to live a life of purpose.

4
Destined to Be Free

When you figure out who you are and start believing in yourself, setting boundaries and living your life to the fullest, those who were just temporary, those that were just using you, envious of you and talking about you behind your back will start to disappear and that's okay. That is what you want, the ones who stay are the ones who love and support you unconditionally, those are your people. Embrace them and love on them.

I have found over the years that loyalty is rare, if you have a set of friends that are loyal, savor it, and appreciate it. It seems that so many people will turn their back on you and use you with no regrets, that is why setting boundaries is important. Saying "no" for me at one time was so hard. I wanted to be liked; I did not want to disappoint anyone even when I was disappointing myself. I was definitely not living free. Because I was unable to say "no", I committed to things that I did not want to do and so often went overboard for people who would not do the same for me.

I am not saying to not to help people, but what I am saying is to be mindful of who you are helping and how it affects you. Begging anyone for a friendship is not an option, and certainly giving when it is ultimately hurting you is a big "no". One thing that I love is when relationships flow easily, that means it was meant to be, you were destined to meet and be friends. I believe that God places people in our lives for a reason and if you pay close attention you will know who He sent to last a lifetime. They are the ones that uplift you instead of putting you down. They listen with no judgement and keep your secrets instead of spreading it to the next person. The ones who push you to be greater than your right now and into your freedom to live destined.

These are the people who set you straight respectfully (and lovingly) when you want to give up or are even in the wrong. I personally do not have many people that I consider to be a friend but the ones I do have I am grateful for the few I have. I trust my circle and that matters to me. It's not the quantity but the quality of friendships and those friendships are part of the freedom to live a destined life.

I am destined to be free.

5
Destined to Live in Peace

Peace will always be my ultimate LIFE goal. living a life of peace brings so much more to your life that includes happiness and contentment. Peace is freedom from overbearing thoughts or emotions, something that is quite often hard to acquire but not impossible. The possibility of living a life of tranquility, free from worry, stress, and anxiety, who wouldn't want that? That's peace. Once again, no one else can give you this but you. It is important to find what brings you peace, for me a nice walk usually does the trick or being creative in some way, from decorating my home to a coloring book.

You must find a way to find your peace, it could be listening to music. I hear that dancing can take you to a whole different world mentally. What about reading a book, connecting with other positive people, affirmations? What's also important is that once you find that peace within yourself to never allow anyone to take that peace away, sometimes it seems as if as soon as things are going well that's when all havoc breaks loose and people try to destroy what you have built, manipulate you into believing your something that you are not, and bringing you down. That is just a trick of the enemy to test your level of peace. Do not be fooled.

Another sure way to find the peace you deserve is through forgiveness, it is not realizing how much forgiveness can lift weight from your shoulders. Forgiveness is when you decide to let the hurt, the resentment, the betrayal, the heartache go in order to find peace. When you realize that your final destination is peace you will find the determination to move forward, not for them but for you. You can forgive someone and never give them access to your life again, you can forgive someone and set boundaries in which you will never let them cross, that is completely up to you but you must forgive in order to heal your heart. It is not easy to forgive, it does take a lot of courage, just like it is not easy to say, "I'm sorry." Whether it is admitted or not it is sometimes that we are the ones that need to be forgiven. I cannot honestly say that I have never hurt anyone, whether it was intentional or unintentional, we all make mistakes, if we did not, we wouldn't be human. It is having the ability to say own up to what has been done and fix the problem.

If someone come to you and says that you hurt them, or offended them in some way it is not up to you to prove them wrong but to listen and make amends, one thing that you cannot do is tell a person how they feel, that causes even more hurt and frustration, sometimes we have to think on how would things affect us, the saying goes "treat others how you would want to be treated" that includes what you say to others. I've run across people that refuse to see themselves but can call out everyone else's transgressions or issues and it is usually the same issues they have.

When you can stop and reflect on yourself and the flaws that you possess, that is incredible maturity and growth and I applaud you. Once again that takes courage.

I am destined to continue to grow and being able to forgive people that have hurt me in my past takes growth because there was a time when I couldn't, cutting someone off was my healing process but it was not a healthy one, once I realized that forgiveness is what will completely set me free, that is what I gave, forgiveness. It even takes a lot of growth, strength, and courage to forgive someone that cannot accept it. I had to forgive my abuser without actually speaking to him because he is no longer living but the moment I was able to forgive him in my heart the hurt was released and it brought me so much peace. Forgiveness is powerful that is why you must never let anyone have that much power over you.

Peace is not negotiable and we are all destined to have it, the work just has to be put in in order for you to be aware of when something comes about to try to destroy it.

I am destined to forgive me and others and live a peaceful life.

Affirmation Interlude

Still Standing with a Broken Heart

When you have a broken heart it can feel like your chest is being stomped on, that its beating uncontrollably or that it is literally crushing inside of you, it can be one of the worst feelings you have ever experienced, it is unbelievable how being hurt can make you feel like you are dying on the inside, I have even heard it said that you can actually die from a broken heart because they never healed from the pain of loss. I can share this with you from experience and I can empathize with anyone going through heartache because a broken heart can make you feel like life for you is over. Heartache doesn't only have to come from a romantic loss but can also be from the loss of someone through death or just a friend that you have been close to that you are no longer attached to.

Sometimes our hearts can be broken from our own expectations, we can often expect more from people than what they are able to provide us. Even when they show us what they can offer we still can expect them to live up to what we see in them or hope that they will change. Unfortunately, only one person can change a person and that is themselves.

Sometimes the Pain is Part of the Process

I can remember when I was going through the pain that I vowed, "it will never happen to me again because I will never allow it", well let's just say that was not the case. I have been hurt, I have felt used, I have been betrayed, I've been let down and all by people who I thought had my best interest. I could have become bitter and declared to never let anyone else in my heart, I promise you that sometimes I feel that way but that thought disappears immediately because I know that there are still good people in spite of the ones that did not see the best of me, through all of it I still healed because I had the desire to get through whatever was breaking me and you can too. I refuse to let anyone take away the best parts of me because they could not see my worth and neither should you.

When I think of the things, I have been through in my life and the times that I thought I was losing when I was actually winning, I become amazed. The changes I have made by force where actually making me a better person and putting me in a position to be successful, when I thought I was falling apart it surprises me how I was actually being set up for greater. Sometimes it is not until you take a breather and sit back and think about what you have accomplished in life that you become grateful.

We can think the world is falling apart around us when in actuality, everything is coming together. Mindset is Everything, even when you think that nothing is going right in your life, you feel that you are losing more than your gaining something good can come of it if you just think about the positive in the situation, there is always something positive within every day even if you just think on the fact that you woke up this morning, that is a blessing in itself. I am destined to find the best in every situation because I know that things could be another way.

6
Destined for Understanding

Hurt people, hurt people. I've heard this statement a gazillion times and I wonder if it is always true, because I can admit that I have been hurt many times and I still have never had the desire to hurt anyone else. To intentionally hurt another person is oblivious to me. Why would someone want to cause another person any form of pain, but I guess it is not for me to know because if I did that would make me one of those people. I am yearning for an understanding.

Who invented "Hurt"? I sure wish I could have a serious conversation with them, out of all the emotions hurt is the one I seem to be most familiar with. There are so many different forms of hurt, there is physical, mental, and emotional. I am not sure which hurts the most or which heals faster, maybe physical because there is usually a specific timeframe associated with physical pain. For example, if you break your leg you go to the doctor and put your leg in a cast for a few weeks and once it is removed you may be as good as new, with emotional pain you never know when the hurt will end, but it will end. Hurt does not last forever. Once you become determined to get up and put in the work to mend your broken heart the hurt will start to fade.

I almost feel like I am an expert when it comes to being broken hearted because I have had some serious heart breaks. When you have been broken hearted you feel like the pain is never ending. A broken heart can set you back in horrible ways, it can make you feel that your heart is collapsing but it is not, and your heart will heal. A broken heart may hurt tremendously in the beginning, but you have to believe that you will be okay.

Although when you think of a broken heart, you think of a failed romantic relationship, but a broken heart can also come from the loss of anyone that you love, family or friend. I know firsthand that it takes time to heal, healing does not happen overnight when you are grieving the loss of someone who will never return or in any capacity. You must be patient and persistent in your efforts to go through the grieving process and heal.

It pays to have an understanding, an understanding as to why someone would want to hurt another person, especially a person that they claimed to love. The best I can do for an understanding is to understand that everyone does not have a pure heart and if they are incapable of having empathy for others and thrive off of causing others pain it is actually hurt within themselves and has nothing to do with anyone else, the best advice is to stay away from people who benefits from hurting others in order to ease their insecurities and pain.

I am destined to understand how everything is working for my good.

7
Destined to Live through Grief

I think the first time I felt hurt was when my mother passed, although I have lost people prior to her the loss of my mother felt different than any of those deaths. My mother died when I was 12 years old, at that young of an age I did not even know how to handle that kind of pain. Lashing out did not help, avoiding the pain didn't help, and for a while neither did talking about it. I was even too young to understand my mother's suffering or to be of much help but later in life unfortunately I had to watch my brother go fight the same illness, cancer.

I remember the day I found out my brother had cancer just as clear as I remember my mother sharing with me that she was diagnosed with breast cancer so many years before, it hurt the same. I worried but I had hope that my brother would fight it and be okay but that was not the case, he did not survive, cancer took my family once again. Although my brother knew he was dying he still stayed positive or himself I should say. The last few weeks of his life he still seemed to keep us entertained, he was much known for trash talking that never ended, he was still himself up until the last night he was with us.

It is amazing how God works and how my brother knew that his time was coming close to an end, he began to say as it got close to his death that he wanted to go "home", he was tired of going through the pain. I can still see the night we prepared him to go to hospice and how he reached for my Dad's hand and held it and he cried, that hurt because we all knew that would be the last time he would see my Dad. He would say to me all the time "I'm the first born" and I would say "I know and I'm okay with that." The last time he said it to me he added "I'm the first one out of here" all I could say was "Don't say that" but I knew it was true, that hurt. Leaving him alone in hospice felt strange, I was so use to him being home at my Dad's. It was as hard from me to leave when I would leave him there too. I would tell him a few times before I would actually leave, "I'm leaving" by the third time he would say "You ain't gone yet?" that meant "Andrese, it's time for you to leave, get out".

The last night at Hospice, a nurse entered the room and asked who was staying and my brother quickly spoke up and said "She is leaving, He is leaving, She is leaving" as he pointed to each of us in the room so we weren't confused as to who he was kicking out. Who knew the next morning that we would get a call to gather the family because there was a change in his condition, and it was time to say our good-byes.

He left this earth surrounded by the people who loved him. I can promise you that the hurt of losing a loved one never goes away, it just becomes easier to bear.

It hurts tremendously when you lose someone even if it is someone that you are not close to, but they were still your family. The acknowledgement or the fact in knowing that you will never see them again whether it is once a year or every day brings a sense of sadness regardless of your relationship.

I've lost many in my lifetime, especially as a young child. I remember losing my grandmother then shortly after my Mother, it almost as if death became normal to me. I think that is why to this day I almost fear it because I know it's inevitable, we are only here temporary and your loved ones are just borrowed, in knowing that we must learn to show love an appreciation at all times.

To survive means to live through something.

I am destined to survive through loss because the loss of a loved one should give me even more reason to want to live, to share the life that they lived with the ones that they left behind that are too young to remember them and even to those that haven't even been born yet. I also strive to make them proud. Yes, loss hurts but it does not have to be the end of your living. What I've learned from loss is that the pain never goes away it just gets easier to bear and you just know that you have to survive.

My brother and I were not the closest considering the difference in age, so we did not grow up together. The most I remember as a kid was him being in the military, so I did not see him much and when he came home of course he lived his own life and did not reside with us. I do remember being so proud to call him my brother even up to his death. I spent more time with him during his illness than I probably did in the 40 years of my life. I am so grateful that I had the opportunity to do that because if I did not, I can't imagine the hurt and regret I would feel right now. Although, there were no ill feelings towards my brother, I think it is important that everyone repair broken relationships because you never know when their last breath will be and you do not want to live regretting not fixing your relationship or at least leaving it in a positive manner.

When I lost my brother, it hit hard and other than the fact that he is no longer here, what bothered me most about my brother's death is that cancer hit home once again; how watching him transition reminded me of my mother's death. You can live through grief and heal to a certain degree after the loss of someone close but it does seem to me that there will always be grief triggers, something that reminds you of who you loss. This is what happened with me when losing my brother and why it felt like losing my mother all over again.

I was young when my mother was sick, but watching him made me wonder what she went through and it is almost as if I was watching her die with my own eyes as an adult all over again. Having to grieve once again doesn't seem fair but we must not question

God for He knows what is best, He always has a plan and the last say and He will get you through the grieving process.

A grief trigger is anything that can remind you of a loss, the memory can come unexpectedly with no effort at all, it can be upsetting for some in the beginning but eventually the reminder of the person you lost will bring you happiness and a smile instead of a frown and tears, from my experience this is when you have accepted that they are no longer here and you are capable of moving on, not forgetting but remembering and moving on with your life.

I am moving from broken hearted to breakthrough; I am destined to live through my grief.

8

Destined to be Healed

It is unfortunate that someone hurt you but that someone is not the person that is trying their hardest to give you the love that you need now so why is it that you allow them to pay for the mistakes and hurt that someone else caused. We can often sabotage our current relationships because of the hurt that was caused in our past relationships, this is not fair to your current mate nor to yourself. You deserve to be free from your past and that includes toxic relationships, that toxic relationship damaged you so you must heal from that pain and stop giving the one that did not appreciate you control over your life by keeping you from accepting the love that you are deserving of from someone else who is not only capable but wants to do the job.

There are some who do not believe that they are worthy of love, respect, and appreciation because someone brainwashed them into believing so, or because they have been disappointed so frequently that they hold themselves accountable for the heartbreak and they feel unworthy, but trust me you are deserving of all of it. You were let down in the past by someone who did not love you. Love does not hurt or disappoint, it does not make you feel less than, worthless, or unwanted. Love makes you feel supported, cared about, safe and adored.

It is often when we have never received these things we feel that it can't be true or that it won't last, you're waiting for them to do you wrong just as your significant other did in the past. I have to be honest, I have felt this way too because I have been in relationships were it was absolutely perfect in the beginning and then it turns, so I know that loving sometimes is taking a risk; but I do believe there is real love out there just waiting to show you and I all that we are deserving of it.

In order to do that sometimes we have to let down those walls we've built up in order to protect our hearts from hurt, harm and danger. I know letting guards down sometimes can be hard to do, I understand more than you know. I have vowed to never let anyone else in my life, no one else will ever get the best parts of me ever again, that I would just be mean and bitter and just show aggressiveness because I didn't want that pain of being hurt ever again, then I realized that I wouldn't be me. Keeping yourself guarded can sometimes only cause damage, we are all meant to love and to be loved.

Heal from that toxic relationship so that you can experience healthy love, once you become confident in yourself, you'll learn to set boundaries and those boundaries will replace that wall, because of your confidence you will not allow anyone to disrespect or hurt you. Heal and keep moving forward.

How did I heal from a toxic relationship? I lived through every emotion, I cried when I felt sad, I yelled when I felt angry, I wrote out my thoughts and my feelings so they wouldn't stay trapped in my head. I talked to someone who could relate to what I was feeling to vent and air it all out. As you start on the journey of wanting to heal, every day gets easier, eventually you will no longer feel sadness, the anger will suppress, and the hurt will soften and disappear. Time heals, at least in my case, it has.

You know you have healed when that person starts to come back around, and believe me, if you were a good person to them they will and you will feel nothing, you will not even want to be involved, you would have grown so far beyond them and more confident in yourself and what you deserve that they won't even phase you. That's growth and healing; congrats you are capable of moving on.

You are destined to find the love that you deserve, and you will be open to accepting and receiving it.

I am healed of my hurt.

9
Destined to Move Forward

When the enemy cannot attack you, he attacks the things that are around you in order to get a negative response from you while trying to prove that he is still in control of your mind, your thoughts, and your feelings. I have experienced moments recently where it seems that he tries to bring back into play what it is that I got myself out of to try his best to break me. Sometimes it takes me a minute to realize that these are the tactics of the enemy and get myself back together. I refuse to go back to a place that I left. I refuse to let anyone, or anything make me feel inadequate. I refuse to allow my temperament to go back to the way that it was, where I was angry, confused, and hurt. I fought too hard to reach a level of peace and I am almost there; I am not going to allow anything to take away the fact that I am growing.

The enemy doesn't like progress, he wants you to stay stagnant, to feel bad for yourself, to not move forward in a positive manner. There are days when I still get sad, emotional, depressed because I for a minute forget what is important in my life, there are some things that I miss to be honest and sometimes that causes me to forget what I have and to enjoy every moment. I always say, "shift your focus" and that is because it works for me. I am still growing and learning, one thing I know for certain is that not all days will be happy ones but not all days will be bad ones either. It is okay to have a bad day, feel sad for a minute or two but never unpack and live there, find ways to brighten up your spirit, do something you enjoy, sadness will only last for as long as you allow it to. If you allow yourself to feel down for too long, you've allowed the enemy to win and that is what he wants, he wants to win but you cannot let him, you must stay focused on where you want to go in life and fight back when he tries to attack.

Affirm yourself by repeating "I am more than enough" or "I am stronger than you" or any other "I am…" that relates to your situation until you feel confident in yourself and you believe what you say. Think of how far you've come. Write out your thoughts so that they are not trapped in your mind, it helps. You are destined to get through the enemy's attacks on your life because you are stronger than him.

I am destined to move forward, past my past and past anything that tries to hinder my progress.

Affirmation Interlude

Still Standing Strong

When it looks like everything around you is falling apart and you continue to stand strong, this is just proof that what you are doing is working for your good and the enemy is mad. Therefore, he is going to try to throw everything at you to make you feel like you are inadequate, that all your hard work is useless, and do anything in order to throw you off of your path of success. He will try to make you feel that whatever it is you are working towards will fail, this is to make you feel hopeless, to cause you to lose your motivation and your desire to accomplish your goals and to live the best of your life and so that you will give up, but don't, instead notice them as distractions and use those moments to push harder and to fight wiser and stronger.

My son once told me that I am not strong as I use to be, although he meant physically, I gave him the response of "I only get stronger" and I meant that in every area of my life. What you may not realize is that every trial, every battle, every downfall is strength training and when you train, what happens? You not only gain strength you gain hard rock muscles and that muscle becomes your shield, with that shield you are able to block those attacks that try to block your path to your destiny, if they come too close they will not hurt you because you have that hard muscle that will lessen the pain and that strength that is going to push you harder.

Finding Yourself

It takes courage to find yourself, to tell the truth about who you are, and the mistakes that you have made and the lessons you have learned from them. Finding myself gave me a sense of freedom, when I got to the point of "what others think of me does not matter", I felt a sense of relief and freedom in a way that I cannot even explain to you. For so long it seemed as if I had lived in the shadows of someone else, hiding the way that I felt, and not speaking up for myself.

The moment that you find your voice you will wonder why you waited so long. The moment that someone stops talking for you and you are able to speak up for yourself your self-worth will skyrocket. It took therapy for me to learn to live for myself and not for everyone else around me, I am even talking in a sense of being a wife and a mother. My family was my first priority which is fine but you have to find yourself in the midst of being a mom and being in a relationship because you are more than just a mom and wife, girlfriend, fiancée, or whatever your role is.

If you are with someone who is trying to stop you from being who you are or pursuing your individual goal, there is something not right about that relationship. I believe that you should be able to work on your goals together and your individual goals when you are in a relationship with the support of your other half.

When you are trying to develop yourself, healthy relationships are important for your self-esteem and your well-being. I've come a long way in finding myself, the things that I enjoy, and just simply liking me. You can do the same.

10
Destined to Positively Impact Others

Do not allow the hurt of your past to stop you from getting the best out of your future. We can shy away from the unfamiliar in life or from something new because we are afraid of what could go wrong by basing it off what happened in the past, this can include relationships. If a past relationship did not work out, we can measure everything that happens in our new relationship by what happened in the old one without giving the new relationship a chance to develop. We can try so hard to protect our heart from being broken again that we may miss out on an opportunity to build an incredible relationship with someone else because we refuse to give it a chance, but how will we ever make an impact on others if we do not give ourselves a chance?

Do not allow insecurities, fear or doubt keep you from what you deserve and that is to be loved, nurtured, and cared about. Always look at your past as a lesson, whether it is admitted or not a past relationship teaches us, what you do with those lessons are completely up to you. Past relationships should build you in some way, it should have created something new in you, if not it wasn't worth your time at all in the first place.

In a past relationship of mine I learned to always take care of myself in a high class manner - to treat myself to the best often - and even after the end of that relationship I still hold on to that.

To make an impact means you have a strong effect on someone else, to be an impact is a major responsibility and an honor. To be able to give something back is an incredible feeling. To create an impact, share your story, you never know who is going through the exact thing that you went through and seeing that you were able to grow and heal through that experience can give them hope, strength and determination to do the same.

How can you make an impact on an individual or even the world? Be kind, be supportive, help someone who is less fortunate, and just make a difference.

I am destined to positively impact everyone I encounter.

11
Destined to Be the Best

We will never be perfect no matter how hard we try, it is an unachievable goal, but giving it your best shot will always be important and your best is an achievable goal when you have the determination and drive to go all in. I am for certain there are many that have tried to be perfect at everything they touched, and it only caused you problems, this is because in my opinion it is extremely unhealthy. Realizing that perfection is not obtainable will lessen stress, anxiety, depression, low self-worth, and frustration. Realizing that you gave it your best will give a sense of accomplishment and satisfaction, but it must be your best. It is also important to know that everyone is different, so comparing yourself to someone else's best is another no, no.

We all have different gifts and talents, we have different ways of dealing with struggles and accomplishing goals, we learn differently, someone may accomplish the same goal that you have for yourself faster than you but that does not mean that you will not get there, it is not a race or a competition. Sometimes we give our best and we still fail, but that does not make you a failure, especially if you gave it your all. When you give your best and you feel that it is not good enough that is when you need to step back from the situation, reevaluate and decide whether it is worth the fight or not. I have found that there are some things that are simply not worth the time and effort if it is causing more anguish than pleasure.

Let's talk about relationships. If you can honestly say that you have given all that you have in a relationship and it was not enough for your partner, do not accept that as a failure. What was not good for one person will be more than enough for someone else, and even go beyond that and just find pleasure in being okay if it is not.

When I first divorced, I felt extremely ashamed, I felt that I had failed and I didn't want people to know that I could not hold my marriage together, but I eventually got out of that mindset and accepted it as a lesson learned. I remembered the fact that it takes two and accepted that not all things work out the way we hope or dream for them to and if it doesn't work just let it go and try again, don't take it as a failure but a lesson learned. I even think back on why does it matter how other people view me or my situation so I no longer feel ashamed, I would much rather live for me than off of the views of someone else or continue to try to fix something that just is not working.

It takes courage to let something go that you have been holding on to for so long or something that is supposed to last forever like marriage when there are so many different factors involved to include what you have built together such as a home, cars, bank accounts and most importantly children. I had to rebuild from the ground up and start from fresh after almost 20 years when I did not think that I could. To be honest I did not think I could go out and buy a new house and I was skeptical about my kids having to change schools but I jumped out there and everything worked out in a positive way, it happened to work out well for them too.

I have always said and will continue to say that God has blessed me when I felt I was at my lowest and I am so grateful for that. Never think that you can't rebuild your life or even what you possess. Never think that you cannot move on or that things will not get better, they always will if you stay consistent, resilient, and persistent and give it your best. I have to admit that my best does not always look the same, there are times when my best wasn't the best. I decided to go back to school after taking a break when I knew that I could not handle the extra load or responsibility. Once I felt that I could, my life changed again because of loss. I had just returned to school when my brother died and mentally I was not ready to take on school but I also knew I couldn't give up the classes. Needless to say I failed because my best at this time wasn't the best and that does happen. But once the stages of grief started to subside I got back in it and although I have to retake those courses, this time around I am giving it my all because I do want to accomplish this goal; and a temporary setback will not dictate my ability to press on despite the pain.

There are many lessons that can be taken from my story to include, you can still prosper after you hit a snag in the road. Don't stop pursuing your goals and believe that you can still flourish even after you have literally failed.

I do not know if we are born with motivation and resilience or if it is something that we learn over our lifetime. It is not always easy to keep pushing when you feel like everyone and everything is against you and you feel that you are alone and there is no one to turn to when you have big decisions to make but sometimes that can also be a good thing, not that you are alone but that you do not share your plans, you lessen the risk of being discouraged because unfortunately not everyone will want you to accomplish your goals or be successful. I can remember when I started to write my first book and I shared the information with one person and their response was "what do you have to write about?", that was the only person I shared the information with, I never mentioned it again until I gave them my finished product.

I could have been discouraged and stopped right there but I did not, and I continued to write and finished my goal on my own. Sometimes it is best to refrain from sharing your business until it is ready to share with the world, it is a fact that you may still have naysayers, but let that be and continue to proud in yourself and your accomplishment.

Validation from others is not required, be confident in yourself and stay in the game even if there is no one in the stands cheering you on, learn to be your own greatest cheerleader. I have always tried to encourage, support and cheer on other people and I am sure that you have to, turn that same energy that you give to others around on you and cheer for every accomplishment. I learned to look back on what I have accomplished and focus on the fact that I overcame with or without support and I am still standing.

Sometimes I don't give myself credit for how far I have come until I look back and actually see how far I've come. There are times when I had to stop thinking negatively and say "wait, if I got through that, why can't I get through this." I went through abuse, were I was dragged, stomped, ridiculed in front of people.

I can still remember the time when I was dragged out of my car and beaten in a parking lot, to get out of a position as detrimental as abuse and still be able to build up my self-worth shows that I can fight through anything. I have learned to not be ashamed of what I have been through but to be proud of that I have overcome. When you shift your mindset to think positive of your situations your whole perspective changes and you no longer focus on the stress and disappointments that you had to face to get to where you are just be proud that you made it to where you are because there are some that did not.

I am destined to always be proud of me. I am the best me I can be.

12
Destined for Happiness

Happiness is a state of mind, a positive emotional state, it is something that you do, it's being at peace with yourself, enjoying your own company, it is all about your personal well-being, it is of course often said that you cannot be happy with anyone else if you're not happy with yourself, is that entirely true, that I cannot answer but I do know that you have to find happiness within yourself, no one else can make you happy overall, meaning you have to be happy as an individual, when that other person is not around you still have to feel satisfied. I am all for healthy, happy relationships but I do believe that you must work on together goals as well as individual goals with each other's support to feel complete.

I at one time had the state of mind of "When I get this…" or "When I achieve this…", I'll be happy. I thought once that goal was achieved that it would bring happiness for a moment but then what? I have heard money brings happiness, money does matter but it is not the only source of happiness and just like anything else it will just bring temporary happiness, the newness will wear off. Finding gratitude in what you have is what builds happiness, finding gratitude in little accomplishments brings me so much joy that is why I can appreciate what may look so minimal or small to someone else. Give me a rose instead of a dozen, I'll appreciate the thought.

When you stop and just be grateful and appreciate everything you will learn to be happy. I am still on the adventure of true happiness; happiness is not something that you try to find or strive to be but an attitude and an adventure that will bring a smile. I promise you that I am not happy within every day and smiling sometimes can be hard to do.

I am almost positive that being happy all the time is not possible, but I am learning to appreciate the moments and be grateful for what I have and what I have accomplished and in return that will bring happiness.

Be mindful of what you give your time to, time is something that you will never get back and not everyone appreciates how precious it is. There was something that I wasted years of my time on, something I knew in the end wasn't going to be worth it. But being the determined person I am, I still gave it my all and stuck in there in hopes that things will turn around for the good, until I knew it was time to give up.

One thing about me is that I will give it my all, that is why I have no regrets in the things that I do, more than likely I will learn something from it because there is a lesson in everything, whether you want to accept the lesson or not is up to you, but I promise you in the future I will be more mindful of what I invest my time in because I have no more time that I desire to waste.

I am destined to be happy within myself and share that happiness with someone else.

13
Destined to Win

When I hear the word win I automatically think of playing a game, something that is competitive amongst a group of people, a sport, or a board game or some sort of competition where you win a prize for being the best but I am actually speaking on winning at life itself where your only competition should be against yourself, striving to be better than you were on yesterday.

What does it actually mean to win? Does it mean you have to be good at something naturally or with practice? What about actually winning at life? How do you know when you are winning at life? All justifiable questions. My definition of winning is simply getting it right. Winning is defined as being successful or victorious in let's say a race. But winning at life means you are living life on your own terms; you are genuinely happy with yourself and your accomplishments. Let me share with you the qualities of a winner, it is have self-discipline, self-direction, a positive level of self-esteem and belief in yourself, all the things that you are destined to have. To win at life, you must not be afraid to fail, stay focused on your goals and desires, have an ambition to learn, and take responsibility for your own actions. Learn that life is not a race or a competition, we are all destined to win. It is a good idea to celebrate the wins of others because you would want them to celebrate your win. Remember that just because you can't see it now doesn't mean it is not going to happen, you must have faith and believe in the possibility that what is for you is destined to come to pass.

I am destined to win because even if I do not win the battle physically, I've learned from the experience so in reality it is still a victory. I will celebrate the wins of others knowing that mine is just around the corner.

I am destined to win.

14
From Affirmations to Declarations

When one is destined for greatness, they follow their own path, conquer their goals, and make their dreams reality. They must believe in themselves and their abilities, even without the validation of others.

To some being great means to be good at something, some may say it is all about having power. To each its own, but to me greatness is not about having power or how good you are at something, but it is all about what you do with it. Greatness can correlate with praise or gratification, some may think that greatness can only be obtained by those are famous or well known or are showered with money, riches, and golds but that is not true. Greatness can lie in the most ordinary person, a janitor, or a teacher even someone who has nothing at all, they are some of the most influential people and they are not famous. When I think of greatness, I think of how one can positively influence another, to me that's greatness. To be great doesn't mean that things in life have always gone your way, the greatest people in the world have had some struggles and still came out on top and are willing to share their hurts with you, why? To change your life.

How does one become great? That's simple, you have got to want it, you have got to want to work towards being better at whatever it is that you want to be successful in. You can accomplish anything that you put your mind to by staying focused on your goals.

Destined for greatness

means that You are not alone. Sometimes when we go through trials and tribulations through life, we feel like it is only us, that we are the only ones going through it and everyone else in the world has the most perfect life. Although you may feel this way that is most definitely not the case. Everyone goes through something whether you believe it or not, whether they admit it or not, it may not be the same thing that you are going through at the time but everyone has test and trials at some point in their life that they have to get through just like you.

Unfortunately, life is not always fair for everyone. I have had to myself realize that I am not the only one going through a loss of a family member, that I am not the only one that is divorced, that I am not the only single mom in this world, and that I am not the only person that has been abused. It is helpful to find others that have been through what you are going through, this helps with healing and growth. When you take the time to see that someone else went through your same storm and came out okay, it will motivate and inspire you in knowing that the same can happen for you.

If they went through that same storm that is trying to take you out and they are still standing so can you. If they healed through all that mess so can you. It helped me to connect with someone who had been abused when I was healing from the abuse, it helped me to connect with someone who had been divorced when I was going through the breakup of my marriage. Sometimes it takes being vulnerable and finding a trusting person to start you healing process so that you can feel whole again. No matter how much you may feel like you are traveling this path alone, you are not alone.

I am destined for greatness because although life has been rocky I still persevere because I know that there is better ahead and my desire is to not keep it to myself but share my testimony and let others know that greatness is within them too.

Repeat after me:

I am destined for Greatness!

About the Author

Andrese has always been inspiring others to reach their true potential regardless of their circumstances.

Her inspirational quotes on social media became so popular that she was encouraged to write a book by her colleagues. Her book entitled "Still Standing" is a testimonial of overcoming.

She is an author, a life strategist, and motivator whose desire is to uplift and empower others to be the best version of them while continuing to grow in her own gifts. Just by living life, Andrese has gained knowledge in how to deal with challenges including the loss her mother to cancer at the young age of twelve, depression, low self-esteem, domestic violence, divorce, and teen motherhood. She thrives by the quote "Resilience is Key". Andrese found her voice not too long ago and released her first book, "Still Standing", in early 2019 with an expanded version "Still Standing: Affirmations of Victory" later that year, in which she shares how to overcome unfortunate circumstances that come about in life as well as her own personal story of grief, low self-esteem, and abuse.

Andrese continues to share her story through motivational speaking and inspirational writing in hopes of uplifting others. She thrives off teaching affirmations because she believes that with practice you can change a negative thought into a positive one. Andrese received her degree in Psychology with a concentration in Life Coaching. She is the founder of Empowered to Inspire, the platform used in order to help others who have been abused and those who may deal with low self-esteem, build confidence within themselves and push past their past hurts in order to maneuver through life. Within the past year she has had the privilege of participating in forums relating to domestic violence, interviews on various podcast and radio shows, writing articles for magazines and motivating others through speaking engagements. Andrese plans to continue to strive in 2020 by continuing to bring awareness to domestic violence and mental health as well as some other areas she would like to pursue to give back, this is just the beginning.

Andrese was born and raised in the Washington Metropolitan area. She is a proud mother of 3 and enjoys reading, writing, and spending time with her family and friends.

 *Stay connected with Andrese*

www.empoweredtoinspirenow.com

Instagram:

@empowered_to_inspire

Facebook:

Andrese Johnson Empowered to Inspire